Rosa
PARKS

Don't Give In!

by Cathy East Dubowski

CONSULTANT
Dr. Erica R. Armstrong
Assistant Professor of History
University of Delaware

BEARPORT
PUBLISHING COMPANY, INC.

New York, New York

Credits
Cover, © Bettmann/CORBIS; Title page, Taro Yamasaki/Time Life Pictures/Getty
Images; 4, Don Cravens/Time & Life Pictures/Getty Images; 5, Library of Congress
Prints and Photographs Division Washington, DC; 6, AP/Wide World Photos/Horace
Cort; 7, Library of Congress Prints and Photographs Division Washington, DC;
8, Doreen Spooner/Keystone Features/Getty Images; 9, Library of Congress Prints
and Photographs Division Washington, DC; 10 (both), Library of Congress Prints
and Photographs Division Washington, DC; 11, The Granger Collection, New York;
12–13 (both), Landmarks Foundation of Montgomery, Inc.; 14, Anthony Potter
Collection/Getty Images; 15, The Granger Collection, New York; 16 (left), Library of
Congress Prints and Photographs Division Washington, DC, (right), AP/Wide World
Photos; 17, Library of Congress Prints and Photographs Division Washington, DC;
18, AP/Wide World Photos/Gene Herrick; 19, From the Collections of The Henry
Ford; 20, Don Cravens/Time Life Pictures/Getty Images; 21(left), AP/Wide World
Photos/Gene Herrick, (right), Alabama Department of Archives and History,
Montgomery, Alabama; 22, Howard Sochurek/Time Life Pictures/Getty Images;
23, Don Cravens/Time Life Pictures/Getty Images; 24–25 (both), Library of
Congress Prints and Photographs Division Washington, DC; 26, AP/Wide World
Photos/Joe Marquette; 27, Penny Weaver/Southern Poverty Law Center.

Editorial development by Judy Nayer
Design by Fabia Wargin; Production by Luis Leon; Image Research by Jennifer Bright

Library of Congress Cataloging-in-Publication Data
Dubowski, Cathy East.
  Rosa Parks : don't give in! / by Cathy East Dubowski.
    p. cm. — (Defining moments)
  Includes bibliographical references and index.
  ISBN 1-59716-078-4 (lib. bdg.) — ISBN 1-59716-115-2 (pbk.)
 1. Parks, Rosa, 1913—Juvenile literature. 2. African American women—Alabama—
Montgomery—Biography—Juvenile literature. 3. African Americans—Alabama—
Montgomery—Biography—Juvenile literature. 4. Civil rights workers—Alabama—
Montgomery—Biography—Juvenile literature. 5. African Americans—Civil rights—
Alabama—Montgomery—History—20th century—Juvenile literature.
6. Segregation in transportation—Alabama—Montgomery—History—20th
century—Juvenile literature. 7. Montgomery (Ala.) —Race relations—Juvenile
literature. 8. Montgomery (Ala.)—Biography—Juvenile literature. I. Title. II. Series:
Defining moments (New York, N.Y.)

  F334.M753D83 2006
  323'.092—dc22
                          2005006173

For more information, write to Bearport Publishing Company, Inc.,
101 Fifth Avenue, Suite 6R, New York, New York 10003.
Printed in the United States of America.

1 2 3 4 5 6 7 8 9 10

Table of Contents

A Day Like Any Other

December 1, 1955, was like any other day in Montgomery, Alabama. Rosa Parks got off from her job as a **seamstress**. She bought some things at the store. Then she climbed on the Cleveland Avenue bus to go home.

Rosa Parks

In those days the South was **segregated**. Laws kept blacks and whites apart. African Americans could not eat in many restaurants. They had to sit in the "**colored**" section at the back of the bus.

Rosa sat down at the front of the crowded colored section. Soon the white section filled up, too. Rosa sighed. She knew what would happen next.

Until the 1960s, Jim Crow laws kept blacks and whites separate in restaurants, theaters, schools, buses, and trains.

5

"I'm Going to Have You Arrested"

When the seats set aside for whites filled up, black people were supposed to give up their seats so that white people could sit down. "Let me have those front seats," the white bus driver called out.

Sometimes drivers made black people pay their fare at the front of the bus, get off, and then board the bus by the back door.

Rosa was tired, but not from work. She was tired of giving in to laws that weren't fair. Three other black people in her row got up. Rosa made a brave decision. She chose to stay put.

"I'm going to have you arrested," the driver warned.

"You may do that," Rosa answered in a polite but firm voice.

Her actions would spark a **movement** that would change America.

Black people could get arrested if they didn't follow the Jim Crow laws.

Whites and blacks had to drink from different water fountains.

Rosa Learns About the World

Rosa McCauley was born in Tuskegee, Alabama, on February 4, 1913. Her mother was a teacher. Her father built houses. Her great-grandparents had been slaves.

Many people, like Rosa, picked cotton to earn money.

On a farm, everyone in the family had chores, even the children.

Rosa grew up hearing stories from her grandfather about how badly slaves had been treated.

When Rosa was two, she moved with her mother and baby brother, Sylvester, to her grandparents' farm in Pine Level, Alabama.

Rosa was smart and loved to read. She spent time fishing with her grandparents, and sometimes she picked cotton to earn extra money. She also helped her grandparents on their farm, where they grew vegetables and raised chickens.

Something troubled Rosa, though. She was beginning to see that black people and white people were not treated as equals.

Separate . . .
But *Not* Equal

Black and white children were not allowed to go to school together. The black schools were poor and open only five months a year. The nicer white schools were open nine months a year.

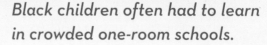

Black children often had to learn in crowded one-room schools.

Rosa saw that some people were mean to her just because she was black. Once a white boy tried to hit her. Rosa picked up a brick and said she would hit him back! The boy ran away. Rosa went home and proudly told her grandmother. She was hurt when her grandmother scolded her.

Soon Rosa understood. Black people could get in trouble for standing up to whites.

The Ku Klux Klan, or KKK, was a secret group of white men who terrorized blacks, Catholics, Jews, and foreigners.

The members of the KKK wore hoods to hide their faces.

Off to School

When Rosa was 11 years old, her mother sent her to Montgomery Industrial School. It was a private school for African-American girls. The school was started by Miss Alice White and other white teachers from the North. Sometimes Rosa helped pay her fees by dusting, sweeping, and emptying wastebaskets.

This teacher's center sits on the site of the Montgomery Industrial School.

Students at Montgomery Industrial School

Rosa learned self-respect and **dignity**. "We were taught to believe that we could do what we wanted in life," Rosa later wrote.

When Miss White's school closed, Rosa once again attended black schools. Then her grandmother and mother got sick. Rosa dropped out of school to take care of them.

White people who helped black people often faced trouble, too. Miss White's school had been burned down twice before Rosa enrolled.

Rosa Joins the Fight

In 1931, when she was 18 years old, Rosa met a man named Raymond Parks. They had long talks about how unfair life was for African Americans. Raymond did more than just talk, though. He had joined the NAACP—the National Association for the Advancement of Colored People.

The NAACP was the first group ever formed to work for **civil rights** in the United States.

Inside an NAACP office in 1945

In 1960, members of the NAACP staged a "sit-in" in Greensboro, North Carolina, to protest segregated lunch counters. At the sit-in, black protestors sat down and refused to move.

The NAACP worked for civil rights and helped African Americans who were in trouble. Sometimes the group had to meet in secret. Rosa admired Raymond's courage. They were married in December 1932.

Rosa went back to school to get her high school **diploma**. She also joined the Montgomery NAACP and became its secretary.

The Desire for Change Grows

During World War II (1939–1945), black soldiers fought bravely for their country. When they came home, they thought life for black Americans would be better. Instead, soldiers like Rosa's brother, Sylvester, were treated just as badly as before.

People worked harder than ever for change. At last, in 1954, the **Supreme Court** declared segregated schools against the law.

Black soldiers during World War II

Thurgood Marshall was one of the NAACP lawyers who argued the case against school **segregation**. In 1967, he became the first black justice on the U.S. Supreme Court.

Black and white children playing in a classroom in Washington, D.C., one year after segregated schools were declared against the law

On December 1, 1955, Rosa got on a bus after work. She recognized the driver. He had ordered her off the bus before. Usually she tried to avoid this driver's bus. She had already paid her dime, though. So she sat down.

"Why Do You All Push Us Around?"

When Rosa refused to give up her seat, the driver called the police. One officer asked her why she didn't obey the driver. Rosa said, "Why do you all push us around?"

"I don't know," the policeman said, "but the law is the law and you're under arrest."

When Rosa was taken to jail, officers fingerprinted her and took mug shots. Then they locked her up in a cell.

The bus that Rosa boarded has been restored and is on exhibit at the Henry Ford Museum in Dearborn, Michigan.

Rosa was taken to jail. Friends came and paid her **bail**. Her trial would take place the following Monday.

That night Rosa's friend, E. D. Nixon (from the NAACP), asked if he could use her arrest as a test case to help change the laws. Raymond was afraid for Rosa, but Rosa wanted to try.

"Don't Ride the Bus on Monday!"

Word spread about Rosa's arrest. Almost three-fourths of the people who rode the buses were black. What if they **boycotted** the buses? What if they all stopped riding? People handed out flyers that said, "Don't ride the bus on Monday!" Black **ministers** preached about the boycott at Sunday services.

During the boycott, black people walked, took volunteer cabs, or formed carpools to get to work.

Rosa as she climbed the courthouse steps

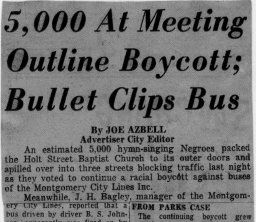

This article about plans for the boycott ran in the Montgomery Advertiser *newspaper on Sunday, December 4, the day before Rosa went to court.*

5,000 At Meeting Outline Boycott; Bullet Clips Bus

By JOE AZBELL
Advertiser City Editor

An estimated 5,000 hymn-singing Negroes packed the Holt Street Baptist Church to its outer doors and spilled over into three streets blocking traffic last night as they voted to continue a racial boycott against buses of the Montgomery City Lines Inc.

Meanwhile, J. H. Bagley, manager of the Montgomery City Lines, reported that a bus driven by driver B. S. Johnson, apparently was fired on by a person with a .22 caliber rifle in the Negro Washington Park area.

Bagley said the bullet hit the rear of the bus and Johnson could not determine from where it was fired.

FROM PARKS CASE

The continuing boycott grew out of the arrest and conviction of Rosa Parks, 42, 634 Cleveland Ave., Negro seamstress at a department store here, on a segregation violation count.

The conviction of the Negro woman may cause a court test

On Monday, December 5, the buses were almost empty. The black community had joined Rosa's fight! Rosa walked up the steps of the courthouse, her head held high. She was found guilty of breaking the segregation laws. She was ordered to pay $14 in fines. Rosa knew the fight had just begun.

"There Comes a Time . . ."

That night a young minister named Dr. Martin Luther King, Jr., spoke to the boycotters. He said, "There comes a time that people get tired. We are here this evening to say to those who have mistreated us so long that we are tired—tired of being segregated and humiliated."

The Montgomery bus boycott made news around the world. Soon African Americans in other cities, like Birmingham, Alabama, began their own boycotts.

The Reverend Martin Luther King, Jr., helped lead the Montgomery bus boycott.

After the boycott, reporters photographed Rosa Parks (center) sitting near the front of a bus.

The bus company refused to change, so the boycott continued. It was not easy. Many people, including Rosa, lost their jobs. She got angry phone calls and hateful letters. Someone bombed Dr. King's house. At last, over 300 days later, the Supreme Court ruled that segregation on buses was against the law.

Rosa Works for Change

The Montgomery bus boycott was a great victory. Laws were changed. Rosa knew, though, that it would be even harder to change some people's hearts and minds.

After the boycott, Rosa couldn't find a job. People still sent her hate mail. At last she, Raymond, and her mother moved to Detroit, Michigan, where Rosa's brother lived.

In 1964, President Lyndon B. Johnson signed the Civil Rights Act. This law ended segregation in all public places in America.

Rosa stayed active in the civil rights movement. She attended peaceful protest marches. People always wanted to hear her story. In 1965, she began working for John Conyers, an African-American **congressman**. One of Rosa's jobs was to help find homes for poor people.

In March 1965, people of all races protested unequal voting rights for blacks by marching from Selma to Montgomery, Alabama.

The Mother of the Civil Rights Movement

Over the years, Rosa continued to work for civil rights. She wrote several books about her life. She received many honors, including the Eleanor Roosevelt Woman of Courage Award and the Presidential Medal of Freedom. Cleveland Avenue was renamed Rosa Parks Boulevard. In 2000, Rosa attended the **dedication** of the Rosa Parks Library and Museum.

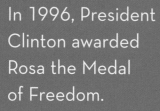

In 1996, President Clinton awarded Rosa the Medal of Freedom.

Rosa's courage changed the world for kids everywhere. These teens from the Georgia School for the Deaf use sign language to say "I love you" as they gather at the Civil Rights Memorial.

Rosa Parks has been called the "mother of the civil rights movement." Her story continues to **inspire** people of all colors to stand up for what is right. Most importantly, Rosa showed the world that one person can truly make a difference.

Just the Facts

■ When Rosa first saw water fountains marked "Colored," she wondered if the water came in colors. Only later did she learn that the signs had nothing to do with the water, but the color of a person's skin.

■ Rosa and Raymond Parks never had children. However, one of Rosa's favorite jobs was working as a youth counselor for the Montgomery NAACP.

Timeline

Here are some important events in Rosa Parks's adult life and in the civil rights movement.

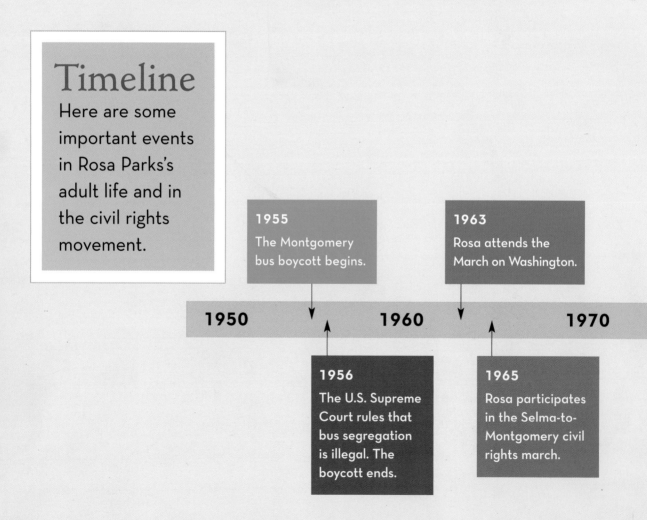

1955
The Montgomery bus boycott begins.

1963
Rosa attends the March on Washington.

1950   1960   1970

1956
The U.S. Supreme Court rules that bus segregation is illegal. The boycott ends.

1965
Rosa participates in the Selma-to-Montgomery civil rights march.

■ Several months before the bus boycott, Rosa received a scholarship to go to the Highlander Folk School in Tennessee. For ten days she went to civil rights workshops with people of all races and backgrounds.

■ During the boycott, the bus companies lost lots of money. Montgomery stores lost money, too. Black people stopped riding the buses downtown to shop.

■ In 1999, Rosa received the Congressional Gold Medal of Honor, the highest award given to a **civilian** by the U.S. government.

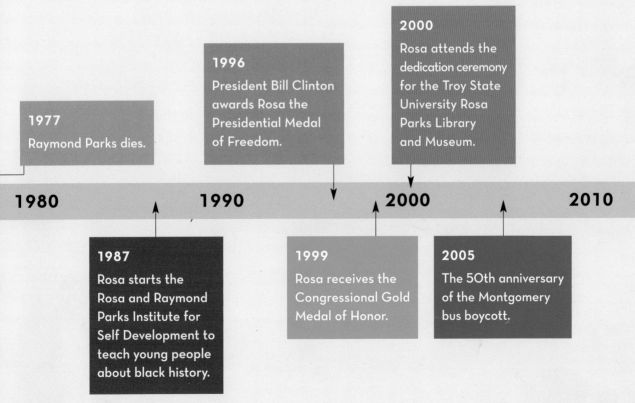

1977
Raymond Parks dies.

1996
President Bill Clinton awards Rosa the Presidential Medal of Freedom.

2000
Rosa attends the dedication ceremony for the Troy State University Rosa Parks Library and Museum.

1980   **1990**   **2000**   **2010**

1987
Rosa starts the Rosa and Raymond Parks Institute for Self Development to teach young people about black history.

1999
Rosa receives the Congressional Gold Medal of Honor.

2005
The 50th anniversary of the Montgomery bus boycott.

Glossary

bail (BAYL) money paid to a court to let a person out of jail until his or her trial

boycotted (BOI-kot-id) refused to buy or use something as part of a protest

civil rights (SIV-il RITES) in the United States, the certain rights people have under the law, such as the right to vote and the right to equal, fair treatment

civilian (si-VIL-yuhn) a person who is not in the military

colored (KUHL-urd) the term many people used in the 1950s for African Americans

congressman (KON-griss-mun) a member of the House of Representatives, one of the government bodies of the United States that makes laws

dedication (*ded*-uh-KAY-shun) a ceremony marking the opening of something newly built, such as a building or park

dignity (DIG-nuh-tee) a sense of honor and self-respect

diploma (duh-PLOH-muh) a paper showing that a person has graduated from a school

inspire (in-SPIRE) to be a good example and encourage others to do something

ministers (MIN-uh-sturz) people who lead religious services in a church

movement (MOOV-muhnt) the actions of a group of people working together to support a cause

seamstress (SEEM-struhss) a woman who sews for a living

segregated (SEG-ruh-gay-tid) set apart or separated from others

segregation (seg-ruh-GAY-shuhn) the practice of separating people by groups, especially by race

Supreme Court (suh-PREEM KORT) the highest court in the United States, made up of a chief justice and eight associate justices

Bibliography

Brinkley, Douglas. *Rosa Parks.* New York: Viking Penguin (2000).

Parks, Rosa. *Rosa Parks: My Story.* New York: Dial Books (1992).

Read More

Adler, David A. *A Picture Book of Rosa Parks.* New York: Holiday House (1995).

Greenfield, Eloise. *Rosa Parks.* New York: HarperTrophy (1995).

Parks, Rosa. *Dear Mrs. Parks: A Dialogue with Today's Youth.* New York: Lee & Low (1996).

Stein, R. Conrad. *The Story of the Montgomery Bus Boycott.* Chicago: Children's Press (1986).

Learn More Online

Visit these Web sites to learn more about Rosa Parks and the civil rights movement:

montgomery.troy.edu/museum/parksbio.htm
www.rosaparks.org
www.splcenter.org/crm/crmc.jsp
www.teacher.scholastic.com/rosa/index.htm

Index

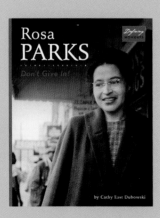

About the Author

CATHY EAST DUBOWSKI has written many books for children and adults. She lives in Chapel Hill, North Carolina.